Path of the Soul

An Anthology of Poetry

Edited By Mark Lane

δ

Published by Dogma Publications

Dogma Publications 4 Overstrand Close Bicester
Oxon OX26 4YP England

Path of the Soul

Cover picture taken from Albrecht Altdorfer's
Landscape with Path
c. 1518
National Gallery, London

First Published 2005
by Dogma Publications

ISBN 1-84591-006-0

Printed in Great Britain for Dogma Publications

Path of the Soul

Contents

A Butterfly Inside Of Me	Natasha Liu-Thwaites	1
In Search Of You	Nilofar Hossain	2
Memories	Anne M Gibson	4
The Unopened Door	Rachelle Mole	5
Fate	Peter Morris-Webb	6
Mountains Of Glencoe	Alma Hynd	7
Flying Circus	Stephen Todd	8
Walking The Dog	Joan Defraine	9
Unicorn	Joanne Alison George	10
Lovehate	Cherry Mom Sen	11
You Dirty Rat!	Jenny Parish	12
The Wonder Of A Sunset	Phillis Green	13
Nature At Its Best	Brid McGillycuddy	14
Inspiration	Pauline Green	15
One Day	Shirley Chapman	16
Peace Of Mind	Sue Handoll	17
Happiness	Gaynor Cartwright	18
You Entered The World	Doris Daniels	19
Reflective Thoughts	Beryl Stone	20
My Fair Lady	Hannah Murray	22
Ice On Fire	Terry Pratley	23
So Called...	Sophie Petrie	24
Strawberry Fields	Michael Linn	25
Imprisoned	Rachel Jane Kelly	26
Dreaming (Of Love)	Barri Lang	27
Youth	Ellen Jones	28
Transition	Louise Holden	29
To Be Awake	Joseph Scarrott	30
Persuasion	Kathleen Bartholomew	31
The Blackbird	John Bowler	32
Passing The Buck	Margaret Power Burnip	33
This My Plea	Graham Allaway	34
The Stranger	Laura Lamarca	35
For Eternity	Dawn Coser	36
The Sweet South Derry Air	Tony Mitchell	37
Deconstruction	Tristan John	38
A Spring Day In The Purbeck's Hills	Sammy Davis	39
Take Me Back...	Christiana Oppong	40
The Stained Glass Window	Jennifer Miller	41
A View Across The Fields	Robert Brooker	42
Tree Blossoms	Douglas Withnall	43
Parting...	Rowena Haley	44

Contents Continued

Our Family Ring	Margaret Thompson	45
Carmen	Richard John Metcalf	46
A Child In The Dark	June Davis	47
The Daisy	Jeanette Niven	48
Hymn	Paul Bett	49
The Wild West	Dawn Morris	50
Canis Sapien	Stephen McGowan	51
He Is Old Now	Michelle Mountford	52
The Darkest Hour	Sarah Newton	53
The Cry	Jen Soulsby	54
I Was Not There	Alan Rowley	55
Spring	Maurice Bagley	56
Alone	Christine Smith	57
Hay On Wye	Andrew Drury	58
Swallows	Jim Lawes	59
Trauma	Tony Reese	60
The Ring	David William Fisher	61
The Meeting	James Heath	62
Practical Magic	Jeoff Newton	63
If Only	Clifford Chambers	64
Lilies	Alison Sutton	66
The Slaughter Of Innocence	Andrew Philpott	67
July Bugs	Antony Hateley	68
Inside Out	Karen Winch	69
Strawberry Blonde	Megan Brand	70
Annabel	Lisa Rolls	71
Shipwrecked	Mark Ritchie	72
An Unnecessary War	Richard Sharpe	73
Your Love Held Me Fast	Jessica Warren	74
I Am A Poem	Lau Thiam Kok	75
A Mother's Love	Pauline Mayoh-Wild	76
The 'One' For You	Sharon Tregoning	77
While Women Weep	Marjorie Nye	78
The Mine	Trissie Burgess	80
Grandad	Maggie McDonnell	81
Empathy	Sean Anderson	82
Expressionless	Lucy Quarrier	83
Morphine Milkshakes	Graeme Robbins	84
Come To Me My Angels	David Boyce	85
A Lesson Learnt	Arthur Frederick Newman	86
My Dreams	Nikita Marshall	87
God	Rabindra Mishra	88

Contents Continued

In This Life	Monica M Baxter	89
Smile	J Clark	90
Life And Love	Alan Unsworth	91
The Bluebell Wood	Judith Kelman	92
Mindful (1)	Dawn Newton	93
My Prayer	Kim Matthews	94
Friends Indeed	Edith Blagrove	95
Seal Of The Wind	Sheila Cheng	96
Spring	Mary L Murray	97
All I Want...	Nargas Abdullah	98
Imagination	Cara Louise Thorner	99
Saved	Shirley Small	100
2am Lonely	Beverley Morton	101
Look Up	Grace Hoggan	102
Hope Of The Rising Sun	Nik Litherland	103
Just Grains Of Sand	Kathy Hirons	104
Revolving	Ann Penelope Beard	105
Heart	Shell Heller	106
Maddy Rose	Olwen A Essex	107
Undesired Growth	Mark O'Callaghan	108
A Smile Sunrises	Nicholas Paton	109
If I Was Born Again	Iavor Lubomirov	110
After All This Time	Michelle McSorley	111
When Love Has Gone	Mary Lidia Evans	112
The Round Of Wrongs	Keith Chalmers	113
Nature's Call	David Thomas Cox	114
Returning Her To Rome	Antony Owen	115
Whirlpool	Pat Ryan	116
The Memories	Laura Bunn	117
Getting To Know You	Charlie Middlemass	118
Crazy Wars	Dessie Carabine	119
11	John Blackburn	120
Every Time I See You	Georgina Blyth	121
Forces	Joseph Nthini	122
Follow The Rainbow	Barbara Holme	123
The Bennett's Old Boatstore	Jim Ravenhill	124
Cheerfulness	Gillian Morgan	125
The Way You Make Me Feel	Laura Edge	126
A Good Day	Rodney Kane	127
Little Bells	Susan Whitfield	128
The Window	Gareth Evans	129
Waves	H J Griffin	130

A Butterfly Inside Of Me

Inside me something spins a yarn;
Cacophonous, no longer calm.
As if a butterfly within,
Moves, lithe, beneath the layers of skin.

This butterfly inside of me,
Fluttering softly, silently,
Awakens when I think of him;
Starts its dancing and beats its wings.

I see his smile and want to weep;
My butterfly will shrewdly keep
The thought of him inside my heart,
Imprinted there, a tender mark.

His eyes are beauty, flecked with green,
Like butterfly wings rarely seen.
His warmth and humour most of all-
My butterfly adores this jewel.

I know the distance, know how far,
It seems to be to reach this star.
I know he's like a boxed-up gem
Closed off to me; no flower, just stem.

I know that I will never hold,
And feel his heat, or break my cold.
Yet if my mind to such thoughts dives-
It keeps my butterfly alive.

Natasha Liu-Thwaites

In Search Of You

The seeds of my journey disperse
across the wild moors,
green with their murmuring.
In dusk's lonely hour,
my unfettered love trails
the starry winds that
call to you.

Who was not with me there?
Staring, as we did,
across the silver spate,
as far as the flowering heather.
That night we took
the road that stretched
towards the hills
in the windless air.

Your semblance of peacefulness,
hidden from my eyes,
tarries across the sedge bank
as you absorb my potent tremors.
I know you are there
in the infinite space beyond;
silent in your mourning.

Come then, to the same place
where you once stood;
this silver moon,
these scented waters,
this silent nook –

The dark grey boughs stir
the wry consonance of the night,
awakening old memories.
Your footsteps tread gently
to the right of my spine
as the weary wind dies
beneath the willow trees;
my heart is unafraid.

Nilofar Hossain

Memories

Within this book, your eye may trace
The well known smile on friendship's face,
There may your wandering eyes behold
The friends of youth, the loved of old
And as you gaze with tearful eye
Sweet memories of the years gone by
Will come again, with magic powers
To charm the evening's pensive hours.

Some in the book have passed the bourne
From whence no travellers ere return
Some, through this world yet doomed to roam
As pilgrims from their native home.
All here by natures power enshrined
As well loved memorials to the mind,
Till all shall reach that happy shore
Where friends and kindness part no more.

Anne M Gibson

The Unopened Door

The day I met you I felt so electric.
The sparks went shivering through my soul.
The pool soft and glistening.
Until you walked through my door.

The door was left unopened, but you still walked in.
Into my life of misery.
You were the outer casing for the inner me.
You were only in my dreams, you were my fantasy.

You came when the stars glittered bright.
You came in the silence of the night.
Migrating souls in flight, carried by mirth and joy.
To foreign skies and distant shores.

The words left unspoken.
The glass door unbroken.
My shattered dreams awoken.

As I grasp the hand outstretched to me.
I feel your presence engulf me
The dream of happiness left untold,
for the emotions embraced to unfold.

Faces no longer sombre.
The enchantment alive inside.
The union of another's happiness
The invitation of love resides.

Having someone to talk to,
someone to whom you can confide.
Sharing intimate moments,
those feelings you have long denied.

My unopened door, now opened wide.
Inviting my radiance to be behold.
My soul entranced with loves vibrance, it's this hand I hold.

Rachelle Mole

Fate

A silent touch, comfort for your shoulder,
A worried heart, warmed by the lips of fortune,
The brittle signs, of one's lost inspiration,
Or that knowing moment, of our predestination,

Whether slipping, forlornly, through the whirlpools of despair,
Or embracing sweet instants, of ever needful hope,
It contrives to enthral us, our lives fragile puppets,
Hanging limply, so helpless, from the twisted twines of chance.

Destiny beckons, our will in our hands,
Favour to the brave, yet empowering the meek,
Racing through time, ever lost grains of sands,
Bound tightly together, in our world run by fate.

We dare not dictate, plan, or find the answers we seek,
But with love, and desire, and a prayer to god's will,
We can see a bright future, and expect what is due,
For we mustn't lose sight, of what destiny brings,
After all, can't you see, it's what makes you, you.

Peter Morris-Webb

Mountains Of Glencoe

Majestic Mountains tall and steep
The world theatre at your feet.
I have not come with boots and ropes
To climb upon your curves and slopes.

I stand in awe and admiration,
Marvel at your time creation.
As the mists drift ore your sill,
Many million years, stand still.

Giant kaleidoscopes display
Where the sunbeams dance and play,
But with snow layers, grey and white,
You shimmer in a different light.

Cascading trees in Autumn dresses,
Wave their gold and copper tresses.
Where is the heather I can't wait?
I will be home twill be too late!

The mist, that rises from the Lochs,
Giving Mountains, large white socks.
But as it rises up the Glen,
You see their muddy feet, again!

Raindrops fall upon your peaks,
Sparkle, as a stream, they seek.
To mirror stones and Lochs below.
What can provide a greater show?

Alma Hynd

Flying Circus

Michael Palin was an Indian elephant
In one of his previous lives
He doesn't remember the details
Which I guess is no great surprise.

Incarnations just can't be predicted
You can never be sure of your past
And who you will be in your next life
And into which role you'll be cast.

So imagine that you are an elephant
A lifetime or two from today
Who remembers a past life as 'Michael'
And how you'd explain that away.

Your friends would never believe you
Though elephants do not forget
How you travelled the world with a film crew
And all of the people you met.

A Python called Monty – well maybe
But your story is getting quite stretched
Elephants don't fly in a circus
Now that is just far too farfetched.

Stephen Todd

Walking The Dog

I walk my dog for miles and miles
Over lonely paths and fields,
I watch the wheat and barley grow
Before giving up their yields.

The rabbits run, the larks fly high
As country lanes we cross,
The stones are wet beneath my feet
And covered with slippery moss.

A stream ripples, laughing at my side
As the dog goes splashing through,
She leaps and bounds in great delight
Then on to pastures new.

The cows look up as we pass by
And slowly chew the cud.
The crows are nesting high in the trees
In the nearby Long Acre Wood.

With a hacking cry a pheasant lifts,
Startled from it's nest,
The dog gives chase but soon gives up
And lies down for a rest.

I call the dog; it's time for home
And a steaming cup of tea,
A loyal friend scampers by my side
And looks lovingly up at me.

Joan Defraine

Unicorn

I thought I saw a unicorn running through the woods
Perhaps I didn't stop and stare quite the way I should
Its flowing mane and silken coat so shining white aglow
Perhaps I didn't stop and stare quite so hard although.

Just between the reaching branches I thought I saw it fleet
But perhaps I should have tried to take a more discerning peep
It looked so white and beautiful with soft brown misty eyes
But perhaps it was a passing trick of summer's evening skies.

But I'm sure I saw its friendly face and streamlined graceful form
Of which there now seems not a trace but I really could have sworn
Its pretty twisted magic horn placed upon its head
Perhaps I was mistaken though imagined it instead.

They say those things just don't exist except in fairy books
But maybe I could chance to say they haven't had a look?

Joanne Alison George

Lovehate

Barriers are transcended
For the little girl with the big heart.
He touches her, she freezes
She feels the pleasure
He penetrates; she feels the pain and shock.
She leaves her body behind,
Life becomes a dream, she is not in control.

A roller coaster of confusion with mixed up feelings,
Learning not to depend or trust
Innocence has ended.
She is deeply wounded,
Suffering with guilt that is not her own.
Concentration is difficult, always confused.
She truly hates her father, forced to love him.

Perception of love is distorted
Is love hate!
Many men come and go
None stay to be hated
She has a lot of love to give, hate blocks her.
Rejected by her mother, family and society
Life is a meaningless hell.

She only knows how to hate what she loves,
Maturity makes her look back, seeing the pattern.
Longing to be free, brings conscious awakenings,
Overcoming many subconscious fears.
It is never too late to have a happy childhood!
All negatives are turned positive through forgiving,
Awareness grows, a new life begins.

Cherry Mom Sen

You Dirty Rat!

Our pet rat is a kleptomaniac,
hurriedly bounding over the floor
intently surveying, searching for…
something…something he can score
…anything he'll carry back
adding it to his little stack
as our pet rat is a kleptomaniac.

Any trophy, any prize, any shape, any size,
whatever…he doesn't mind, any treasure of any kind,
empty cartons, discarded wrapper,
used up packets and crumpled letters,
dirty tissues, old fag butts, apple cores and yoghurt pots
shiny button, dirty socks, cotton reels and an old matchbox.
Nothing's too good for our pet rat
the seasoned kleptomaniac.

Proudly prancing, almost dancing, nose held high, tail aloft,
trotting slowly, sideways glancing…showing off!
Treasure in mouth, eyes sparkling with glee,
he's silently shouting…
hey! Look at me…
I'm your special talented rat,
The world's best kleptomaniac.

Jenny Parish

The Wonder Of A Sunset

When the day is done, the sun goes slowly down.
Creating an aura of colour like a shining crown,
The rays rise up and paint the sky,
With feathers of gold reaching ever high.

A golden light is reflected far down below,
Creating warmth of colour with its radiant glow.
It shines through branches not burdened with leaf,
A wonderful vision on a Winter's eve.

As the eventide draws ever near
The night sky in the distance begins to appear,
With golden shafts of light streaking through
Like bolts of lightening disappearing from view.

Sinking ever slowly beyond the horizon
Until the glow, has finally gone.
Like the wind on a candlelight that flutters and dies
Leaving an utter emptiness across the skies.

And then an opening up will take its place,
A night of blue sky, with infinite space,
Where the stars of the universe sparkle so bright
At the end of day; and the beginning of night.

Phillis Green

Nature At Its Best

It was a very glorious day
With Nature at its best
We walked and walked
Without thinking of a rest
Birds of every colour
And every different sound
They captured us so much
We had to turn around
Nature is oh so sweet
Where would we be
If we could not see
A Cedar tree.
Or the colours that abound
In the sky and on the ground
That's why we all should live
And be prepared to give
A little help
To nature at its best
So that in harmony and peace
We one and all should live.

Brid McGillycuddy

Inspiration

You are my inspiration
The light in my life.
You are the candle burning
Burning true and bright.
You came into my life
And my life began anew.
Now my world is so happy
Especially when I'm with you.
You are my inspiration
The everlasting glow.
So always stay beside me
For I do love you so.
You are my inspiration.

Pauline Green

One Day

One day a cloud of angels will gather in the sky
and in their midst the Prince of Life, will stand by.
A myriad of trumpets will sound,
for every soul will be found.
Believers will kneel and pray,
To thank God for this promised day.
But those who doubted will feel ashamed and walk away,
And for a thousand years they must repent,
until once more their names, in the book of life are lent,
Then Jesus will walk upon the earth,
to consecrate the word, foretold before his birth.
And when he raises up his hands,
the angels will understand and carry the believers away.
To a place called Heaven - beyond the Milky Way.

Shirley Chapman

Peace Of Mind

What is that little thing called Peace of Mind?
How, when and why does it elude?
Or when it's there' why is it there?
Sometimes to stay for days or not an hour.
What does it mean this little phrase?
A burst of happiness or stillness grave
Or just a thought that winds its way
Through meadows green into melting day.

Sue Handoll

Happiness

Happiness is giving, laughing and living
Caring and sharing, longing and loving
Poetry and flowers, children and song
Birds, bees, animals, pets that belong
Our parents, our children, our brothers and sisters
Our babies and toddlers, wiping tears and their blisters
Dad coming home from work, dirty but happy
His wage packet checked, he's not sad or snappy
Dinner on the table - his favourite food
Mam's eyes glisten - she's in a good mood
Happiness means different things to different people
Our Church, the bells, the spire, the steeple
Contentment, good health, satisfaction, ambitions
Well think! All achievable and all so precious.

Gaynor Cartwright

You Entered The World

You entered the world during the night
With you came a ray of light
For as the dark turned into day
Peace came to an Island far away
Tho' my heart for you is filled with pride
A small corner has been set aside
To weep for Grandmothers who will see no more
Their loved ones left on a distant shore
May you grow up in a world full of love
With God looking on you from above.

Doris Daniels

Reflective Thoughts

Sleepless nights, close to despair-
What I wanted to say I could not dare.

I wanted a life of equal rights,
certainly not one of constant fights.

I felt controlled - no life of my own,
but over the years the seed was sown.

I tried to make my feelings clear,
but inside me there was this fear.

I was too weak to stand my ground-
My inner strength could not be found.

Long ago I should have been strong,
instead, I apologise when not even wrong.

Over the years you would not listen,
So many times my tears would glisten.

What I wanted to say I could not dare
You see, at heart, I did still care.

I wanted to shield you from being hurt
but ended up by being curt.

I dared not say my love has gone,
where once, for you my eyes, they shone
But-
Our love has grown to a different kind-
More tolerant and hopefully, for life will bind.

Throughout the years we grew apart
When and why did all this start?

We'll now amicably go our separate ways
to a more contented and happier phase.

Get on with life, learn from our errors,
Smile and enjoy our next endeavours.

Beryl Stone

My Fair Lady

You, my darling were sent from above,
To teach a man like me how to love,
I love you dearly; you know its true,
For my life would be over if it weren't for you,
Even if we can't be together,
I fear I will always love you forever,
Please tell me you fell exactly like this,
My heart will burst without one last kiss,
Your husband is the luckiest man alive,
I'm trying to move on but alas I strive,
My soul is incomplete without you here,
My life will be no more without you my dear,
So I will leave, go far away,
I'll die and never see another day,
Pretend you never knew me, I was never real,
Pretend I didn't feel, exactly how I feel,
Will you forget that you loved me too?
I'll never forget the way I love you,
Just remember one thing, how it would be,
If we were together, my fair lady.

Hannah Murray

Ice On Fire

Ice on fire
Diamond lights under auburn hair
Seek me out with an angels stare
They can look right through me.

Satellites
Liquid gold in the purple air
Late at night, like there's no-one there
They can see right through me.

Restless wings
Keen to know what tomorrow brings
Learn the meaning of everything
Sense my deepest feelings.

Ice on fire
Ageless stars in a velvet sky
Seek me out in the place I lie
Stay with me 'til the day I die
They can look right through me
She can see right through my soul.

Terry Pratley

So Called...

But a child to the eyes
You walk alone in this disguise
A shadow of some supreme grace
Left when it abandoned this place
The only light renounced to replace
The dark that consumes each life's chase.

Escaped tears fall at your feet
Hiding the rot you make complete
While you shudder at what is left in your wake
And dream of a light you do not hate
The sun still shines down in hope of remake
And chides you for your constant ache.

A little stumble in your walk reveals your detachment
Fear not the possibility of your ruined hearts re-enactment
Your voice screams with a whisper
Masking what your eyes cause to splinter
Heading for a deadlier sin without remittance
As you allow all voices to take hold with acquiescence.

Come; sit a while under the eaves,
The eaves of every fallen dream.
Ease yourself from the ring of your halo,
And take your hands away, so you can see,
I do not fear that you have no face.

But a child to the eyes
You walk alone in your disguise
Sacrifice your wings.

Sophie Petrie

24

Strawberry Fields

You walk in a field and see a strawberry,
Take it, it's for free,
Bite into it and taste the sweetness,
It's a gift from nature for you and for me.

It lies in peace under the sun and in the fresh, clean, tasty air,
The strawberry has no good; its only desire is to share.

The juices of it caress your tongue as if they were meant to be,
A few minutes ago they hadn't even met
but nature is the language we can read.

But as humans have we appreciated this earth's generosity,
Instead of preserving, we've poisoned you with fumes
that destroy and kill.

The air is getting dirtier; the seas are rising high,
the black dust is gathering as the days become the night.

As a black cloud swells over, the once bright, blue sky,
The strawberries, trees and birds all begin to die,
When the world comes to an end, we have no-one else to blame.
We destroyed the things that were given to us
out of greed and with no shame.

The strawberry field in the summer were all the children played,
Is now fenced off and torn up, now roads have been laid,

The apocalyptic black sky that the nearby power station has created,
Shadows over the strawberry field as the last days are counted.

Michael Linn

Imprisoned

The scent of death fills this room,
And to what I see my frightening doom.
As I kneel I'm always a slave,
Always lonely, always afraid.
The darkness swallows my exposed soul,
And the fate of you forced me to fall.
Blinded by fear and wounds so deep,
I gaze at him hard, trying to sleep.
Trying to sleep and never wake up,
Never wake up, never wake up.
Never wake to my tortured being,
But sleep forever, never seeing.
This is my torture, this is my hell,
This is because of the day that I fell.

Rachel Jane Kelly

Dreaming (Of Love)
(To my beloved, you are missed)

She was a vision,
a dream always out of reach.
I knew not her passion
her touch so sweet.

Now I have awoken,
her beauty endures.
Still my dream, still a vision,
but also much more.

For a time my soul sings, it soars, it flies.
Now it screams in unhappy confusion.
My octopus has gone, I sleep again it cries.
Joy is dead, it's departed, a cruel illusion.

Barri Lang

Youth

She dances in the golden light
A tiny form with skin so white.

She smiles and beckons silently
Her wings fluttering in the breeze.

She calls me to my childhood days
A singing memory lost in haze.

I try to follow her darting glow
Though my feet are heavy, my body slow.

I wander far with a heart of hope
Until my will begins to choke.

As darkness falls and cold winds blow
I fear I lost her long ago.

Ellen Jones

Transition
(For Perthshire poet Kenneth Steven - with gratitude)

Happy sad day
No reason to be down
Red rowan September is here
The swallows have gone
And the geese have not yet come.

Happy sad day
The shiver in the breeze
Makes free with August's stolen warmth
This month has made its own
And pretends that autumn's lost.

Ever was I warm and cold
Ever have I lived life old
Yet young, scarce begun
This betwixt-between season of my years.

Happy sad day
This corner of the year
Brings fear of winter's gloomy moods
Yet precious to remember -
There will be only a few days like this.

Louise Holden

To Be Awake

Dreams that haunt me are not always bad,
Identification of them is frustratingly sad.
Containing the life which could have been,
To wake in real time is exceptionally mean.

I used to believe my dreams were some sort of gift,
A psychic ability or mystical earth bound rift.
A postcard that's supposed to be sent,
Containing a message, that must have been bent.
As I have no idea, what it should have meant.

Why do I see things that can never happen?
Why do I show more emotion asleep than awake?
How do I feel more alive in the other dimension?
Yet I reassure myself that it has to be fake!
For those several hours I get a greater sensation.

At least when I'm asleep everyone's there,
My minds a bigger place than the universe,
So there's room for all to share!
And with me as God, no one will see a hand that's unfair.

Reality sinks in and the heart is trampled with air,
I turn on the light and realise your not really there,
Breathing is good but a fading image is torn.
We grew up together since the day you were born.

Why this early for you to be set free?
Oh how I still wish it had been me!

Joseph Scarrott

30

Persuasion

His voice, soft,
Persuades my love, emerge! emerge!
No! Lay sweet, and virgin like
So none can take, and give, that kind of love that danger
Waits to kill.
Hurting now the soft voice says, Adieu!
And then the pulse fades-
It cannot live.

Kathleen Bartholomew

The Blackbird

Oh blackbird I love to see you fly
I love to hear your song with notes so sweet and high.
But when I've raked my flowerbed with so much care and finesse,
Why in your search for worms to eat
do you make such a darned mess?

John Bowler

Passing The Buck

Do flowers have mummies and daddies?
He asked me innocently.
Why are some trees taller than others,
How do shrubs know what colour to be?
Does a willow weep because it's sad
Do leaves hurt when they fall?
Who taught the spider to spin his web and why are ants so small?
When the day is hot and sunny,
How come the breeze is cool?
Do worms really know how to read books?
For I have never seen them at school.

He bombarded me with questions,
I answered as best I could.
About the ways of mother-nature,
He said he understood.
'You know everything',
'You're clever' he said with a smile on his face.
'I know a lot about nature now,
Tomorrow we will talk about space'.
Well I nearly swallowed my tonsils outer space he must be mad.
Tomorrow I am going to busy I said,
You will have to ask your Dad.

Margaret Power Burnip

This My Plea

Let me be and let me bleed,
Let not the wolves upon me feed,
Keep me safe and keep me warm,
Save me from life's cold hard storm.

Let me breath and let me sleep,
Let not these walls around me creep,
Keep me healthy keep me sane,
Save me from this lost love pain.

Let me feel and let me see,
Let not these demons follow me,
Keep me focused, keep me calm,
Save me from some untold harm.

Let me live and let me smile,
Let my heart run free a while,
Keep me straight and keep me keen,
Save me from those fears unseen.

This my plea I offer up
For destiny to fill my cup
Do not fail me do not hide
I need to feel some peace inside

Graham Allaway

The Stranger

One day I met a stranger
Who was unknown to me
He shared his deepest secret
Laid bare for me to see.

He talked of his regrets
Mistakes that he had made
The sacrifice he'd taken
The highest price he'd paid.

I felt his heart, his feelings
The turmoil in his head
His wish to talk to angels
Instead of walking with the dead.

Locked inside a self-made prison
The despair that he called home
No laughter from his heart, no song
He was feeling all alone.

So I gave my hand in friendship
To a stranger who confided in me
That stranger is my friend now
For all the world to see.

Laura Lamarca

For Eternity

There's nothing in this world,
that can compare to you,
you're constantly shining,
through everything you do.

You bring so much joy,
to everyone around,
and inside you there's something,
waiting to be found.

Well babe I think I've found it,
it means a lot to me,
now we can share our love
for eternity.

Dawn Coser

The Sweet South Derry Air

Warm Summer's day on mountain high,
Spread flat squinting at sky and winking at clouds.
Stepping lightly through flower steeped meadow
And luscious glen, with sun on face
When jaunting back again,
And everywhere the embrace of nature's scents.
Football games of note at the 'Screen,
Broad country voices that laugh and scream
As banter of distinction competes.
Trekking from Tirkane 'cross heath and heather
To Ponderosa's feeding,
Mindless of weather as the Glenshane drops quietly away.

Across furze-laden fields of the 'Derg,
The blossoming whins stand out from the grass bedding,
Whilst pins of reeds cluster and jostle on the damper soil.
Religiously stepping to revered Church Island,
Where memories crawl from the stones to gaze
At an evening skyline over Lough Beg where the waters smile.
Nights at the marina, where tentative couples do explore
And butterflies carry you to the waters edge
Where fear retreats before desire's courage.
Whether it be the soft touch of dewy rose
Or her soft dark hair that carries the heart through
The sweet south Derry air,
The strength of the dreams remain.

Tony Mitchell

Deconstruction

Poetry - the ultimate communion:
Two souls meet, momentarily -
Depart upon a journey of two methods
To two destinations -
To guess the hidden meaning in the
Gaps.

And through your inference, guess my implication;
Through knowledge of my inspiration -
Biography the key,
With social history:
A context to explain my words -
And more so the words that I left out
(If I left any out at all).

'What does he mean by this or that?'
 - Parentheses a million times perhaps -
A flick of the pen
'And what   ...   this
A word left out -
Intent
Or otherwise?'
What purpose serves the server well,
With techniques and his

Enjambment - a device to bemuse the second soul?
No the authority is in the second not the first,
Who holds his critical power of solution
And all owed augury acclamation
For how he   fills   the   gaps.

Tristan John

A Spring Day In The Purbeck's Hills

At the breaking of a dawn
On a spring day
The sky was misty and fluvial grey.
And happily I ramble along
Nature's awakening narrow lanes.
I turned a sharp corner
And stood impassively still.
Admiring a patch of lovely primroses,
Some white and some blue,
Yet - so flimsy on the domain
Nestling at the foot of a winding steep hill.
And higher I climbed up
More the magical the views to stare.
And so exciting to be there!
As ones looks down at the sea,
And the sand drifting with the waves.
Steadily washing around the holes old cave
And to see the lilies sleeping
On the placid pond waters.
And gently hanging over the borders
To me-these hills hold many latish
Mysteries of the past,
And always waiting to be re-cast.

Sammy Davis

Take Me Back...

At first I thought I was dreaming
but, no! It's true
I thought I saw your face beaming
but it was a strange hue
Thought I did something wrong
but couldn't figure it out.

It's cold now I wanted you to
step down
      hold me, my Love, my sweet
let me feel the warmth of your embrace.

You seem so distant, so far away
Come back to me: my ONE, my ONLY
Can you hear me?
In a tunnel all I can hear is the words echo back at me.
I'm scared get me out of here...

I miss the light, the warmth, the heat, the smile...
How could my joy cause me pain?
No!

...I'll stand by you...
I made up my mind that once
Tell me something, talk to me love
I'm listening, trying to
Maybe I can't hear

I gave my all, my life, my all, my love
And I'll give it all up again...
For you.

When the storm dies down, that river crossed,
and the night is finally over....
We'll go back to the place we first began.

Christiana Oppong

The Stained Glass Window

Its beauty's far more worthy than words or simple gestures.
The beauty's only felt, far beyond perfection.
The many years of learning,
Working in conjunction with men of art, men of design
To create, rebuild, participate as midwife to a masterpiece.
Each separate piece of unimportance
Stained in carefully chosen colour.
Mounted high in walls of grace,
To reflect the sun, to light the face.
In this peaceful, holy place
A little pride is permitted.
To flow through the veins through the structure and floor,
To walk down the aisle and turn at the door.
To treasure a gift from the living.

Jennifer Miller

A View Across The Fields

As I look across the field I can see a tree.
And high up in that tree there is a bird.
I love to watch the different birds,
They bring great joy to me.
I really like that tree.

As I look across the field I can see a fence.
This fence is very high and grey,
It's razor wire topped al the way.
The razor wire cuts the birds.
I really don't like that fence.

As I look across the field I can see a house.
In the house there's lots of people,
Lots of those people work here.
They look after and watch over me.
I really like that house.

As I look across the field I can see a road.
And that road leads to Oakham.
From Oakham, it goes to Leicester
And Leicester is near my home.
I really like that road.

As I look across the field I can see my future.
In the future is my freedom.
In my freedom I will be better
And in being better I will like myself.
I really like my future.

Robert Brooker

Tree Blossoms

It could be Autumn
And yet it is Spring,
As we walk on a carpet
That's fit for a king-
A carpet of petals
So lovely a sight,
Falling as gently
As dew overnight:
Nature's confetti
Strewn all around
In the wind and the rain
And with never a sound.
Just one more stage
In glorious Spring
For all to observe
That each day may bring
Something new, something old,
To remind us that each
New day may bring change
Well within our reach.

Douglas Withnall

Parting...

Take your hand off my chair
I find it uncomfortable sitting there!

Take your coat down off the hook
I want it gone next time I look!

Take yourself and all your lies
I can no longer look into your eyes!

Take it all and close the door
You don't belong here anymore!

Now you've gone I'll be ok
I will, I will, I WILL ONE DAY!

Rowena Haley

Our Family Ring

January, July
September, November
Five birth stones
for there's two in September.
All making up
our family ring
each stone different
memories to bring.
father, mother, sister's brother
This is a ring
that is like no other.
A gift for a daughter
birthday treat.
A ring that will
always be unique.
One day handed down
to the next in line
so it will be come in time
part of our heritage
part of our tree.
A family heirloom
Forever be.

Margaret Thompson

Carmen

Binoculars; obsessive youthful lust;
A lock of hair and lewd imagination;
Glimpsing underwear; a room with just
The two of us: the perfect situation.

I was strange, hurt and misunderstood.
You a beacon in a stormy sea;
Your fire picked out from stars as best I could,
The crashing water misdirecting me.
I wonder, were you an unwilling magnet,
You adored, a vulpine prey pursued,
I adoring, sounding violent trumpet?
Hunted by my eyes, you were their food.

Years have passed and I return to you,
A needle turning north, a bond like glue,
A teenage landscape littered with desires,
And all of them devour with deadly fires.
But more mature with ripe respect for love,
Yet you I cherish; you I'm thinking of.

Richard John Metcalf

A Child In The Dark

I never did like the dark; it gave pounding unto my heart,
Mind racing to and fro, at that moment nowhere to go.
All things going through my head,
Thinking thoughts, they would find me dead,
Weird sensations all about, my voice gone, could not shout,
What was in my dark at that time, the fear it was really mine,
Knowing something was really there, could not see though I did stare,
Panic I did, not the word, my whole being quivering like unto a bird,
A bird that had lost its way, being susceptible to any prey,
I was in a mess, this I can tell, going through some sort of hell,
Of my beliefs I was not too sure, until I had learnt much more,
Understanding then that they were near, those of heart I held so dear,
My dark now it is so bright, I have that of spirit in my sight,
Lit now is my candle shining bright, no darkness now just full of light,
In my dark I now say a prayer,
Knowing others are there with me to share,
This love and light all times to be, in my life for me always to see.

June Davis

The Daisy

Like a drift of snow on a summer's day
Bright bank of daisies is held in sway
Eyes focused firmly on the source of light
Hypnotically stare with all their might
When the sun appears at the break of day
He touches them gently, they feel him and they
Open white petals and big yellow eyes
Lifting them up to the endless blue skies
Watching all day till the coming of night
The light is no more; they close their eyes tight.

Jeanette Niven

Hymn

Let my soul
  by Spirit fill,
Let my reason
  by subtlety confound,
Let my anger
  by peace diffuse,
Let my sorrow
  through contentment flow,
Let my thoughts
  by contemplation grow,
Let these words
  by beauty show.

Paul Bett

The Wild West

A cry in the distance, an eagle in flight
the motionless landscape stands in their sight
hazy heat all around
lie still while they pass, we can't be found.

With dust on their jackets and an old cowboy hat
they crawl through the bushes steering clear of their traps.
A gun in their pockets and a knife in their boots
their ready for action when the night draws.

The moon rising high brings fear to their hearts
the only sound is a wild dog as it barks
a well lit valley down below
all we need is for the enemy to show.

And at that second a horse comes to sight
with a dozen or more following closely behind
the outline of Indians riding silently at night
means only one thing, it will be a tough fight.

Then a noise behind makes them turn and stare,
at a figure standing with your teddy bear!
It's only a bad dream son, only a nightmare.

Dawn Morris

Canis Sapien

She's condemned to a life of lycanthropy
She with the eyes of a newborn puppy,
With the claws and the jaws of a child of the wild
With the pelt and the scent of the wolf on the prowl!

She's consumed by a life of lycanthropy
She with the fangs of a fledgling vampyre,
With the heat and the hunger of a child of the wild
With the speed and the greed of the wolf on the prowl!

In the paws of the lycanthrope are we
Seduced by our thoughts and on heat for thee,
We lay us down to wait; abandonment is now our fate...
Sleeping with the lamb we wait for '*canis sapien*'.

She comes to me in dreams, to succour me and ease my needs,
Olfactory senses heightened as her hold on me is tightened;
I can almost feel the moonlight by which she hunts...
And smell the ravenous pack that follows her.

'If all beauty be in the eye of the beholder
Then behold her carnelian eyes,
Be enamoured by their guileless stare - as I live now content...
Amongst the fox and wolf, and suckle in their lair'.

Stephen McGowan

He Is Old Now

He is old now, raggedy too,
If I lost him I wouldn't know what to do.
This friend of mine since I was small,
I think I'm going to keep him till I'm tall.
He still feels soft and is kind to me,
Even when others are better looking than he.
I shall never replace you so have no fear,
You are far too precious to me my dear.
Your beady eyes and little nose,
You don't quite hold the same pose.
It doesn't matter, needle and thread,
Quickly done so you don't dread.
Fixed once more, not quite the same,
Not the look of how you originally came.
Never mind, you still are soft,
And will never be thrown into the loft!

Michelle Mountford

The Darkest Hour

In ones darkest hour
One drinks
One smokes
One thinks.

One thinks of ways
One thinks of maybes
One thinks of action.

then the lightest hour
sober
thoughts
the plan
the solution
then in motion.

Sarah Newton

The Cry

I feel
the deep throb of a past
enshrined.
The living pulse now
extinguished.
I see you standing
as sentinels of some great
knowledge
flowing still to the future.
Experiences
unexplained.

You reflect
the shouts and groans of past
earth magic.
Leaving whispers now
empty in the shadows.
You face
towards the dawn
encircling
THE dance of life.
Channelling power
Spanning forwards
upwards, inwards, outwards.

And I hear
the cry in my being.

Jen Soulsby

I Was Not There

I was not there when all around the Christmas spirit did abound.
I was not there when all the snow lay 'crisp and even' on the ground.
Nor did I see the slant, symbolic leanings of the tree.
Fading now such memories have for me.
I was not there; I was elsewhere as children sang as best they could
For coppers they could take away,
For time has come to give them hearing this yuletide day.
My mind goes back when I was young
And for myself I would have sung.
But things have changed, as well they should,
This turning back the clocks no good.
Join in the merry making throng to which it's clear you do belong.
But doubts creep in and so hold sway on situations far away.
I was not there when all about did sing and shout.
I was not there, for the moon was out.

Alan Rowley

Spring

In a blaze of sunlight and little white clouds
It comes
With new green
And snowstorms of blossom
Doors stand open
To allow it in
And it moves unseen through winter rooms
Every second is momentous
Of unspeakable joy
Annual mystery has returned
Season of dark bright green and yellow
The sod shining darkly
Off a gleaming spade
Hark!
Shouting Wren
Who decibels the dawn
With ancient news of hope.

Maurice Bagley

Alone

I like being alone,
It has to be said.
I make my own life,
No one to consider,
I do what I want.
I'm a free spirit,
Ask anyone.
But yesterday,
As I walked through the wood
Its sheer beauty pierced my heart.
I turned to tell someone.
No one was there.
But I like being alone,
It has to be said.

Christine Smith

Hay On Wye

Brown bovines browsing
And the orchard boughs bow
With russets ruby red.
The grass is freshly mown
And the crops are harvested.

In the verdant valley
Nestles a neat restful town,
Where ancient tomes are sold
And past forgotten voices are heard
In fading folios old.

At the cosy cottage
In this autumnal stage,
My soul is scanned by your look-
My emotions a translucent page
In an easily read book.

Andrew Drury

Swallows

The swallows swoop and sweep the sky,
Drop down to dip he pond's still skin;
Disturbing insects dancing nigh,
Yet never hit their hurtling kin.
Their aerobatic, free display
Delights me, lazing in the sun.
Such speed! Such swerve! Such artistry!
The envy of an earthbound man.

Jim Lawes

Trauma

She moves, as in slow motion;
Gasping as she comes suddenly to rest, with heart breaking,
Trauma awaking the grief that lies dormant in her aching breast.
Dark imaginings bode emptiness for her future life!
Like a residue of scar-tissue, in a mind
Rife with tortured memory of golden days, once theirs,
Now gone forever into a black hole of obscurity.
She dreams of what might have been;
Suspended in the mist of borrowed time, with eyes beseeching,
Arms reaching out for something now irretrievable - sublime.
Jumbled reasonings drive the millstone of her crushed despair!
The slow, relentless turning of the wheel
Offers no repair to her ground-down emotions,
Stretched out as sand on a distant shore,
Awaiting confinement to the deepest oceans.
She grieves in silent agony;
Suffering the throes of inner pain, with body tensing,
Mind, dispensing thoughts that have no meaning in her muddled brain.
Distant thunder raises the spectre of his untimely death!
Formal platitudes turn her mind to the horror of his final breath
And to all it would deny her.
'With deep regret'…'Have to inform you'…'Tragic death',
Then the final insult: 'Killed by friendly fire'.

Tony Reese

The Ring

Seven times around the ring I ran,
When the moon went out of sight,
Sure enough, the Devil appeared,
Just as the clock struck midnight,
I drank the milk he offered from a bowl,
And wondered whether he'd grant my wish
Or just steal my soul.
On Midsummer Eve, I saw the fairies dance,
The next night, the glowing lights of spaceships prance,
Then witches gathered to unleash a horror so tragic,
A five-pointed star for a ritual of black magic.
The trees are birdless, and enshroud in a dead slumber,
I tried to count them, but they wouldn't number,
Three times around the Ring I ran,
When the moon was full with light,
A woman on a white horse appeared,
Riding through the night.
Right then, my legs froze, and I collapsed to the ground,
Then there was a strange crackling sound,
An uncanny sense of some unseen presence,
Surrounding me with evil, in essence,
It followed me to where I fell,
I entered the dark wood, and it cast a spell,
The trees took me prisoner, and their branches began to sting,
I had been consumed,
By the legend of Chanctonbury Ring.

David William Fisher

The Meeting

They sat side by side
One with coffee and one with tea,
Tones of superficial politeness falling from their tongues,
The understanding once shard, gone to air,
With perpetual wish to rejoin their long parted folly they meet.

In times gone by they laughed and smiled
With innocent understanding of life's small joys,
And a calm upon both minds eye
Mustered by the sleep they shared,
A double foetal position him in front, her behind.

Loving eyes filled her moon-forged face
With gentle kindness of loves embrace,
A fleeting smile, reviles her lines of laughter
Testament enough to the timeless childlike moments
Both play and pleasure of youthful lust and wonder.

With coffee gone and a tea stained cup
They part to separate bedtime rooms,
And dream of past perfect moments,
The timeless hours and lasting stairs,
But will is work when one drinks coffee and the other tea.

James Heath

Practical Magic

Off I went the other day to meet a witch's daughter
I wanted to learn quickly just how to walk on water.
'It's nice to meet you sir,' she said, 'for knowledge you do thirst
But if you're going to try that trick it helps to freeze it first'.

I thought that I would catch her out then her I would outshine
I said, 'How would I then turn water into wine?'
She fell about with laughter and didn't give two hoots
She said, 'My man that's easy, just get a kit from Boots'.

Jeoff Newton

63

If Only

If I didn't need to work no more
having come into lots of dosh.
Such lovely thoughts of life ahead
those poorer days I'd quash!

If I didn't need to work no more
life so leisurely for me.
The café just around the corner
would be my daily cup of tea!

If I didn't need to work no more
the charities I could help.
It would make me feel so good
To see the odd heart melt!

If I didn't need to work no more
I could travel to many places.
Visiting almost anywhere
seeing many faces!

If I didn't need to work no more
not worrying about enough cash.
Going out to spend willy nilly
and wouldn't need to dash!

If I didn't need to work no more
family would also want a sum.
Friends too might knock on my door
with charities begging for fun!

If I didn't need to work no more
I'd have to be on my guard.
from those who'd keep telling me
that their financial lives are hard!

I've gone off the thought of working no more
I'm fine the way I am!
Keep all my friends and family
and open my tin of Spam!

Clifford Chambers

Lilies

A full 6 leaf starlet of gold
Emblazons the room with its warmth,
Shielding our souls from the cold
Autumn colour, from birth, looming forth.

Each petal arranged like a tear
That's conceived in the duct of an eye,
The stem, long and green, can it hear
Trickling water? Without which it will die.

Stem and buds rejoicing together
And expanding to enlighten our lives;
For a short time, they make inclement weather
Sweet as honey like the fruit of bee hives.

The pollen, as bright as a grapefruit
That's juicy with vitamin C,
Can imprint its bodily offshoot
With more strength than both coffee and tea.

A fragrance, both pungent yet sweet
Emanates the air, which surrounds.
A distinctive impression we greet
From an odour which gently abounds.

Alison Sutton

The Slaughter Of Innocence

When you look in to eyes of the children, what do you see?
A thousand days of innocence, or a thousand days of fear?
Are we witnessing the slaughter of innocence before our eyes?
Every child that encounters hate carries that hate for a lifetime.
For every child who lives in fear, the slaughter has begun.

Every child,
Who lives through the savagery of war, is a victim of the slaughter.
Every child,
Who suffers at the hands of an elder, is being taught to hate.

Every child,
Who witnesses death by the hand of a fellow human,
Is a witness to the death of humanity
Every child on earth has the right to innocence,
The right to live a life free from fear.

We must put an end to the suffering of the children.
For the children are the tutors of the future.
Teach the children tolerance that they may tutor tolerance.
Teach the children understanding that they may tutor understanding.

Teach the children our mistakes,
That they may avoid the mistakes of the past.
Teach the children kindness that they may spread kindness

Teach forgiveness that they might forgive.
Love the children that they may love.
The time has come to hand the children back their innocence.
The world is a wash with spilt innocence.

For the sake of humanity let the children live.
Set the children free.
Our time on earth is short,
Let's use what time we have left to heal the children.
That they may heal the world.

Andrew Philpott

67

July Bugs

All shall hear what's become
Of our fabled bard
A token flash of glittering bugs
To lift this tale above the tard
In symphony
Not unlike lovers on a blessed eve
Whose picturesque embrace
Bids warm air
To all who breathe.

Antony Hateley

Inside Out

My feelings are released,
but my thoughts are trapped.
I know no way of getting them back?

To take a knife,
to watch me bleed,
In my mind that's what I need.

To cut my arm,
to see me bleed.
The red drips of blood,
the comfort I need.

Rip at my skin.
Release the pain.
Wear it outside,
more wounds to hide.

A scab to a scar.
Reminder of who you are.
But the pain on the outside,
is a release from within.

But then the cycle again will begin.
Destroying me slowly from within.
Till I slip and slip and again give in.
Destroying now from the outside in!

Karen Winch

Strawberry Blonde

Light caught the single strand of golden hair
lying on the pillow - I leant over and
traced its outline, the silky touch transporting me

to that moment when all seemed perfect.
Her arms holding onto me, her
warm breath on my neck, my hands stroking
that silky hair which flowed down her back.

Empty.
So rarely now was there any of the feeling,
the feeling that had caused so much pain.
Should I feel guilty? Ashamed? Resentful?
I just feel. Empty. Alone. Cold.

Longing.
for those sensations of love and desire,
of perfection and contentment.
All seemed uneasy and confused -
Uncertain, insecure.

Megan Brand

Annabel

A cry from one soul
Demolishing all fears.

Silence shakes the room
Break the silence breath once more
Open one eye, reach out
Please God let her call out.

A mothers anguish a thousand tears
A cold embrace which should have burnt for years.

She's breathing just hold on through the night
Days to follow of great hope and pain
A thousand more tears begin to rain.

Two years on a child burning bright
Thank God she made it through the night.

Lisa Rolls

Shipwrecked

A lonely ship on a hardened sea
Oh my life come back to me
That wondrous day I found your face
Love at first sight it was the case.

How we grew and then apart
I then perhaps misplaced your heart
Deep fits of anger violence too
Your makeup colours black and blue.

To strike at you to cause you harm
Was outside my normal charm
But what made you want to decide
To move that table to the other side.

You didn't ask I didn't hear
Remember I make the decisions here
So hurry up and pack your life
I need to find another wife.
There's no repair the guarantee's gone
Your love for me was just some con
So close the door leave the keys
After 30 years get off your knees.

I've made the choice its plain to see
You are no longer part of me
Don't contact me that would be wrong
And don't come back you're not that strong.

Mark Ritchie

72

An Unnecessary War

I was born in the sixties,
The Vietnam War.
Haven't we had enough
Of what we saw?

It seems time doesn't heal,
It just helps us forget.
A new generation of power
To kill 'folks' they've not met.

A country invaded,
Surely, would put up a fight.
And decent honest people,
Not understanding, what's wrong or what's right.

Some ones unleashed a demon,
The country was theirs
So a lot more will die
Oh well, Tony, George, who cares?

Richard Sharpe

Your Love Held Me Fast
(For My Mum and Dad)

To the hand of destruction, I lean in for its touch,
Willing to be engulfed in its misery.
As I fade away from limbo to death.
Something holds me fast.
Resigned to the damage of my body and soul.
Blocking out the comfort of a loving tender kiss.
I would rest on the brink before destruction's abyss.
Sensing inevitability, arms spread to plunge.
Something closed around me and held me fast.
Confusion, an ache of familiarity
Chipping at my stony resolve
While my eyes look into the face of resolution,
Something held me fast
Confused and dazed by the power that held me,
Wondering what could meet death and victor over it.
Lowering my arms and as weak as I could be,
My pain though not gone has eased.
As I slip from horrors jaws and step from the void
I saw it was your Love once more that held me fast again.

Jessica Warren

I Am A Poem

We are a piece of a poem
Can be written can be sung
Bridged and unbridgeable
Like the ocean like the sky.

You are a piece of a poem
You are the cloud you are the wind
Touched and untouchable
Reached and unreachable
Like a dream and dreams.

I am a poem
I was the storm
Now I am the river
Melts in the ocean
Looking up at you looking up at you
(Who) sew my words (who) weave my dreams
In the blue land above me.

Lau Thiam Kok

A Mother's Love

When a mother loses a daughter, it's the saddest thing on earth
The love they shared together just kept on growing from birth.

She filled your life with so much love
An angel sent from up above.

Each day you watched her grow with pride
With a feeling of love no mother could hide.

She came to you when she needed a friend
You were always there for her up to the end.

How can you live when she's no longer there?
Her life cut so short it seems so unfair.

Her beaming smile would light your day
As welcome as the blossoms of May.

You remember the lovely times you both had
It would break her heart to see you so sad.

She's gone to a place where she'll suffer no more
One day she will meet her at heaven's door.

Where she'll smile and take you by the hand
To a place they call the Promised Land.

So don't let the heartache spoil the view
Of the beautiful daughter you once knew.

She's there in spirit although you can't touch
But she knows you all loved her so very much.

Pauline Mayoh-Wild

The 'One' For You

You think you've found the 'One' for you.
Everything so happy and new!
Then troubles start and no more love is able to grow.
Drift apart, until the 'One', you no longer know!
So what now, what will I do?
Knowing that part of my life is through!
Sink or swim, live or die.
Or just look back and ask why?
All the feelings felt so secure.
But of them, now, I'm not so sure.
So muddled and confused.
Just feel hurt and so abused!
Have to make my mind up then.
Never want to try again!
Just want to be by myself.
Don't mind being left on the shelf.
I may be on my own, but at least I control my Destiny!
Never going to let anyone, take the rest of ME!

Sharon Tregoning

While Women Weep

Into the bright September day
A spectre of evil stalks its prey
And women weep.

Who does this evil so reviled?
That maims and kills a little child
As women weep.

I see blackened ruins high
Pointing accusing fingers at the sky
As women weep.

Whose demonic hand does this?
What curse of treachery we can't dismiss
As women weep.

It stalked the killing fields in Vietnam
Then through streets of Omah it ran
As woman weep.

And still this evil stalks the land
With that incandescent raging hand
As women weep.

Then deadly torment in Afghanistan
To the slaughter of children in Babylon
As women weep.

And the death of the children in Sudan
Join those of the Chechnian
As woman weep.

And now that hand of hatred does damn
Those gentle children of Beslam
And women still weep.

What difference can there be?
Between these innocents why can't we see
Why women still weep?

Marjorie Nye

The Mine

Standing like a skeleton
Against the sky
Machinery of the old coal mine.

Miners now have long since gone
No sons are there to carry on
The whistle that was once so shrill
Now is quiet, all is still.

Grass grows between the tracks
Where the coal came shiny black
The coal seam is alas no more
No men from below do pour
Into the warmth of the sun
With black faces, hard work done.

Many now are old and grey
And can look back on those days
And feel proud
That they worked for coal underground.

Trissie Burgess

Grandad

My Grandad lived in the middle of the row,
And all his neighbours he got to know,
Who was in and who was out,
Who drank beer or a bottle of stout,
Their proper names wouldn't stay in head,
So he called them by their numbers instead.

To Granny he'd say 'No. 10's not well,'
'And I think 24s about to sell,'
'No. 2 is still in bed,'
'I better check the man's not dead,'
'That 36 should get a job,'
'And her at 8 is a bit of a snob,'
'You're a nosey parker,' my Gran would jest,
'Sit yourself down, and take a rest.'

In his faded suit he'd pace up and down,
His hair all oiled, like a man about town,
He was seventy-five and still quite trim,
'That widow at 30 fancied him,'
His working days were over and gone,
But he didn't find his days too long.

He'd check a lock and close a gate,
And rap a window if he thought they were late,
He'd give advice and lend an ear,
Listen to their stories and shed a tear,
'A peoples person,' his work never done,
Till he passed away at eighty-one.

Maggie McDonnell

Empathy

I weep for those with no shelter tonight,
I feel their pain, their agony and their plight.

I weep for those with no one to hold,
To keep them safe and warm in the cold.

I weep for those who run and hide out of fear,
Who get nervous and scared every time someone comes near.

I weep for those who have suffered an emotional fall.
I know where you are at, I cry for you all.

Sean Anderson

Expressionless

She sits and stares,
For hours or seconds
Lost in the whirlwind raging inside.
Time is as motionless as she is,
Maybe it's racing past her again and again.
She cannot tell.
She does not care.
Her identity is her own,
But she does not possess it.
Vivid as the black expanse before her,
Touching her, embracing her, isolating her.
Cruel as her pointed talons
Kind as the softest feather touch.
Stroking the knife before her,
She sits and stares,
Expressionless.

Lucy Quarrier

Morphine Milkshakes

I saw it, in the road ahead
Life's road ahead, from child's eyes.
I saw Armadillo, or some such name disguised,
The sickly sweet, the sickly cheap, a special treat
For his 'three day week' of mind.
I smelt it, on the road ahead, and cared less for it and I,
Through breath a bottle old, credence nullified.
Occasional dislike, grew strength and sinewy roots,
To the bone core bone, to the splitting core truth,
To the wishes, darkened pity, raised on malevolence toast
All the drunkards,
Swilling cheap gin, to the mood swinging punches,
He was bound to win.
I watched it, as gently could,
Those blanket eyes sunk barren grey,
All cheek bone dead, and sent away.
I touched it, lying cold, lying to me about being old,
But morphine milkshakes taste so sweet...
'It', will be dead, within a week.
It barked to me...'I said good-bye!'...
'I love you dad'. 'I love you dad' said I.

Graeme Robbins

Come To Me My Angels

Come to me my Angels,
With wings as white as snow.
Because you mean so much to me,
Although you already know.

Come to me my Angels,
With skin so pure and bright.
Although we know you're always there,
You're always out of sight.

Come to me my Angels,
When I am very low.
Help me through this sad time now,
Because I need you so.

Come to me my Angels,
In the special angelic way.
To relax my mind and body,
As I kneel down here to pray.

Come to me my Angels,
Cos we like to feel you near.
Like white clouds on a winter's day,
With sun shining from the rear.

Come to me my Angels,
With spirit and with love.
Whilst flying here from heaven,
Like a big white turtledove.

Come to me my Angels,
Every time you hear me pray.
Then I know that you'll be with me,
On our Gods calling day.

David Boyce

A Lesson Learnt

If you can make an error, and admit it,
And take the taunts and laughter with a grin,
You're a better man than all your glib tormentors,
For you've proved that you can take it on the chin.

And while they're laughing, you have learned a lesson,
A lesson that is learned by very few,
For you're walking in the footsteps of the mighty,
Because even they made errors, just like you.

Arthur Frederick Newman

My Dreams

Every night whilst I'm asleep
The dreams I have I join and meet:

The little boy that never talks
The king-size bed that's able to walk
The countryside with lots of flowers
The princess in the very tall tower
The tiger waiting for its prey
The elephant as it trots away.

These dreams I only have at night
I am so glad they're not a fright!

Nikita Marshall

God

They say
A leaf doesn't move without Your will.
If so
On whose will
Flies feast on faces of dying infants in Darfur
Mothers cry for mercy in vain
Pain, pain and pain
Some parts are ridden with drought
Others are flooded with rain?

They say
You are the supreme judge.
Then
Why sinners enjoy, innocents cry
Edi Amins live and Dianas die?

Still they say
You are the ultimate truth.

If that is true,
Something is seriously wrong with You.

They think I am a non-believer:
They explain to me about *karma*,
They talk about *punarjanma*,
The wisdom bestowed on human beings
And the follies they commit
All that might be true
But if You have devised such a painful truth
Who else can be guilty?

I am sorry, my Lord,
It has to be You!

Rabindra Mishra

In This Life

Life has been sent from God above
To use in plenty like a peaceful dove.
This beautiful world is full of wonders,
Keep still for a moment while one ponders.

In this life, beauty is in most things
Whether it's classical music or a song of Bing's
Animals and birds are one of my features,
After all they are all God's creatures.

In my life there's no time to get bored,
Play a piano tune or strike up a chord.
My working life is a thing of the past,
Life is busy, but not to fast.

Helping folk brings great reward,
Especially Winnie, Amy and Maud.
When I cannot visit I drop them a line,
I telephone them to know all is fine.

At the end of the tunnel when I've done my lot,
Of all the people I am but a dot.
I'll be thankful to our Lord on high
When He calls for me as the clouds roll by.

Monica M Baxter

Smile

A smile doesn't cost
a lot, if a smile is
all you've got,
for a smile will
help you through the day,
and a smile will chase
all your blues away,
a smile is all you
need to do,
so 'Smile' and the world
will smile with you.

J Clark

Life And Love

Life's a long road
Sadness joy and love
Don't sit round and wait
For things to turn out good.

Find someone you love
To help you on your way
Don't forget to say
You love her every day.

Tell her when your wrong
Stand up and be a man
Give her all your love
As much as you can.

Find someone like I did
A lover and a friend
Love her all the time
And love her till the end.

Alan Unsworth

The Bluebell Wood

A sea of blue beneath
young beech and hazel leaves
fluttering golden and lime green in
the sun, is heaven indeed

Wood anemones peep out at me.
Their faces nodding in the breeze,
against the dark brown leaf litter
of last year's Spring.

I hear the sighing of the trees,
and little birds, their high whistles
enchanting, and comforting in the
quietness of the wood.

There are hoof-prints of tiny deer,
but not a sign of one.
All have fled long before my feet
walked where they had lately pranced.

I sit and soak up all I see and
hear and smell and feel.
Then in the dark days of my future
life, I can return here in memory.

Judith Kelman

Mindful (1)

We forget at some stage that we come in alone
And go out the same way,
Is anyone really free for a day?
Easy to manipulate,
Permission to judge,
We select how we speak,
Points of view hard to budge
Simple so, if we only know how to preserve animal instinct...
Start now!
We go with the flow through the good times and bad, choices,
decisions, consequence mad
Events that occur beyond our control,
Years down the line before we feel cold
Impossible really to turn back the hands,
But it's possible now if we want to make a stand
We fear, we dread, envisage the shame,
Eliminate this and tell of your name
You can't please them, even some of the time,
Release what's pent up, even turn it to rhyme
We're living' life much harder than it really needs to be,
Make use of your trash....
You want to live free?

Dawn Newton

My Prayer

Thank you Father for calling me near
To teach me to love those I hold so dear.
I cherish life so differently now
You've shown me the way and taught me how.
I feel my life's just starting anew
My heart's fully open since I found you.
Please keep on giving strength to me
To pass this on to my family.
To teach them how to love and give
To be a Christian as long as they live.

Kim Matthews

Friends Indeed

There are no riches money wise
But to be content without disguise.
Now eight three years old
Always have a smile I am told.
Which makes me rich in friends
Who are always willing for a chat
Not about folk, but just this and that.
To talk makes one much wiser.

So open your door, go on a bus
This, I find is a must.
Your neighbours are just like you
Waiting for someone to have a brew.
A cup of tea breaks barriers down
So get out there with never a frown
You may find you wear a beautiful crown.

Edith Blagrove

Seal Of The Wind

Over, to the North, I heard, your whistle
Flying towards me, sent from the heavens.
I never lost faith, I never lost hope
Of finding you there, joyously.

You, I shall find, in sweet, harmony
With open wings spread, protecting me.
We'll be together, we'll forever see,
How God planned our love to be.

And even though, dark clouds, will cross our lives
They'll be of, no challenge, we'll conquer them.
United as one, our strength bonded,
A ray of light will eternally shine.

Sheila Cheng

Spring

Spring is nowhere, hip, hip, hooray
What shall I do on this lovely bright day,
Stroll around the garden to check what is growing.
Seeing the fruition of our hard Autumn's sowing.
Or walking through the parks, with their colourful displays
Oh how we've longed for these lovely Spring days.

We awake full of optimism, and gladness that's true
Looking out of the window, see a sky that's so blue,
People feel happy with the beginning of spring
Flowers start blooming and birds start to sing.
Bulbs begin shooting up out the ground
Different varieties and colours are found.

Window boxes, garden pots all full of colour
Arrangements of flowers, complimenting each other,
Now winters forgotten, that spring is now here
The beginning of Spring tells us Summer is near.

Mary L Murray

All I Want...
(For my father M. Abdullah Zaid)

I've made a promise, which I aim to fulfil
It's going to be hard, but I know I'll win.
All I want is this dream to become reality
So my family will be granted the best wish in humanity.

To keep them happy I will always be there
They've done so much for me and I've got to be fair.
I'll face every twist and turn that comes in my way
So I can stand up proudly, clear my throat and say...

'The journey has been hard but I've made it through...
And I want you to know that I've done this for you'.

Sometimes I cry but find it hard to explain
I'm very happy, but still there's pain.
The pain of losing and not getting there,
But there's nothing I can do, life can be unfair.

Despite all this I'm still going to fight
When things go wrong. I'll put them right.
I just hope I fulfil their dreams and reach up high
Before my time is up...before time passes us by...

Nargas Abdullah

Imagination

I imagined our meeting, but never the parting,
I imagined our first date, when true love was starting,
I imagined your parents; we got on so well,
I imagined your brothers they both gave me hell.
I imagined your dog that loved me more than you,
I imagined your sister we went shopping for two.
I imagined our house the way we'd decorate,
I imagined my reaction, when you came home late.
I imagined my future; you have always been in it,
I imagined our past and the happiness in it.
I imagined my traumas you would always play down,
I imagined an emergency you always came round.
I imagined the darkness dissolved by your light,
I imagined you holding me all through the night.
I imagined how we'd be when we were both old,
but I never imagined you'd be so cold.
I imagined you pleading and beg me to stay,
but I never imagined I would be in your way.
I imagined you loved me - I imagined all wrong,
I imagined too much, I imagined too long.

Cara Louise Thorner

Saved

My sins oh Lord, possessed me,
My world was full of doubt.
I longed for peace within me
My life was inside out.
But then I heard the story
Of Jesus and His love
Of how He came to save me
Sent here from God above.
Jesus filled my life with hope,
He took away my fears,
When I felt sad and lonely
He wiped away my tears.
Now my life has peace and joy.
My days are filled with thoughts
Of Jesus and His mercies
And my salvation bought.
Thank you, thank you Jesus
For all you gave to me.
Your life, Your love, Your everything
That day on Calvary.

Shirley Small

2am Lonely

Insignificant little house stands beneath the lamplight
Still and silent shadowed by the night
Behind the lilac door it dwells once again
Lying in the same place since a quarter past ten
Cobwebs dance to the breeze that slips through the window
Behind drawn curtains, candles glow
Steadily ticks the clock that is being observed
Minutes pass quickly like the time already served
The bird's song echoes across the fields as daylight dawns
Rays of sunshine awaken the child who yawns
The waking of the street drowns the bird's song
Lonely lies still, the morning didn't bring a friend along
Nighttime drifted by as quickly as each breath was drawn
As quickly as the years since lonely was born
A gentle breeze flutters the summer leaves, green and limp
None of these beauties aroused lonely from its sleep
Or hid the world from its own ugliness
The bird's song nor lush land had a cure for loneliness.

Beverley Morton

Look Up

The way of life is hard at times, like walking a stony path.
You've got somewhere, achieved something, suddenly it
slips from your grasp with never a hope to succeed.
We only have ourselves to blame if we feel like a broken reed.
What's happened to your spirit as you fought your way to the top?
You still have that spirit - although sometimes forgot.
You remember all the sorrows and are so full of regret
Remember the happy 'tomorrows'
and you'll climb your way back yet.
Look on the sunny side of fortune - there may be little your way
You will find - no matter how-
Dame Fortune does smile your way.

Grace Hoggan

Hope Of The Rising Sun

Is tomorrow merely
The next rising of the sun?
Or is tomorrow the day
When my turn will finally come?

Is the person next to me
Finally the one?
Or will she one day leave me
Like all the rest have done?

Are the numbers in my hand
The ones to change my life?
Or will they once again let me
Stay buried in my strife?

Will the works I've written
Be savoured with every chord?
Or like the others in my life
Will they be ignored?

Will the test I'm taking
Make me fail or pass?
Will I ever be the best
Or have I failed my class?

Do I mean as much to you
As you mean to me?
Do I hold your heart forever
Or will you set me free?

Me, I have to have some hope
On my knees, I pray
The answers I am looking for
Will all be yes one day.

Nik Litherland

Just Grains Of Sand

The man returned before too long,
He now knew what he'd done wrong,
Looked across the fields of maize,
It was all clear, not even a haze,
The sun was up, it had risen,
There was no warmth, only a prison.

All around the men they lay,
Their sons and daughters would wake today,
And think of their fathers far away,
For those the most I can do is pray,
But they can't return to those they miss,
For tears of joy, not even a kiss.

For here are the men who once stood,
I couldn't save them, I knew I should,
But as they faced the enemy fire,
I ran and ran, the legs didn't tire,
I let them down, I was not there,
I was only nineteen, but will they care.

Medals they'll not give to me,
Even though they will never see,
They'll call us heroes, we'll never forget,
But here today our maker we met,
Now as I lay down, pistol in hand,
We really are just grains of sand.

Kathy Hirons

Revolving

Calm in the early morning air,
As the crisp atmosphere wakes.
With the twinkle of the stars,
As sunrises they seem to drift out.

The morning chorus merges in,
Man's eruption blurs everything out.
So much to do, no time to look,
Missing the beauty natures about

An ever moving picture flows,
For the sky and landscape doesn't dye.
Man that revolves the wrong way round,
Finds discontentment why it passes by!

But he that revolves with time,
The beauty of life is found.
And the magic and mysteries unfold,
Why happiness, contentment is sound!

Ann Penelope Beard

heart

if i took out my heart and laid her naked
in among the oak tree roots i could watch
her bleed raw passion into the rigid bark,
knowing that my wild and wanton magic
could at last explode unfettered in a crazy
quantum thrust of joy that would travel up
through leaf to star - unlike the blood on
ancient pyramids that slithered down to
earth from barren stone-faced altars.

if i took out my heart and laid her down to
quiver in your palm i would watch you cradle
her and listen to her fire songs knowing that
you alone would understand the molten sighs
of love that danced and flickered there.

Shell Heller

Maddy Rose

'Oh Maddy I adore you
You are the world to me.
The presence of you near me
Sets my spirit free.

You cheer me when I'm oh so down
And take away my awful frown.
Through telepathic though you show
To what great heights a love can grow.

Your loyalty it knows no bounds
With others I could go ten rounds!
But Maddy you're my saving grace
You're chair it should be decked in lace.

Your eyes are bright, your heart so pure
A nature that will all endure.
Oh precious gift from God of mine
You've truly made my life divine.

Upon each other we so rely
Apart who knows we may well die.
But every day is oh so rich
Now we've found our true niche.

Without you little friend of mine
My heart would ache and I would pine.
As long as you are in my life
I know I'll cope with all the strife.

Your little face so picturesque
Stands so high above the rest.
Your lick of trust - you are burlesque
I surely have been Heaven blessed.'

Olwen A Essex

Undesired Growth

Slowly I fall into a never, never world.
Gripping to the very ropes of my sanity.
Slowly I waste to all as my mind curls.
While the very building blocks can have no pity.
The moving world flashes by with little time to waste.
At my side stand all I have ever lived for.
The embroidered memories break from there holding paste.
They leave me shattered, distant like an old folklore.
Understanding myself has become a thick lonely mist.
Standing alone covered by the clear reality of it.
To bury itself in the dirt of my own madness pit.
Tormented with the confrontation of my own human weakness.
My lack of requests has left me no alternative.
To afraid to ask I crumble inside my own mind.
Nothing is logical yet it all seems so relative.
My only hope is the changing years of time.
That growth answers its own self-destruction.
These learning years have taken all my loot.
My life my dreams my hope of resurrection.
The thoughts of building again all that I have created.
To be robbed and foolishly blinded.
While the thief walks and leaves me devastated.
And I think, well, I still have my mind!!

Mark O'Callaghan

A Smile Sunrises

A smile sunrises
to the surface;
tears, a kiss:
The final echo,
so far, far-flung.

As passing icebergs,
unending bodies unseen,
frozen ages:
Past love past
hope, past pain.

Or windswept worlds,
viewed from the sun
vast continents:
Life, lightening,
lying under cloud.

Just a floating tip,
a teeming landmass,
I am, you are, us all:
Hoping to discover,
to be uncovered.

Nicholas Paton

If I Was Born Again

If I was born again
I'd watch each sunset
I would rise
Each morning for the dawn.

I'd drink in every tree and leaf
Or rock or blade of grass
Would touch each pebble
Take in every cloud.

I'd stop each person that I see
To talk and listen
And try to know
Their joy or sorrow.

If I was born again
But not this life
So busy with its pains and aches
Desires and lusts.

But not this life
Where boredom exists
And complaining stillness
In this dull-eyed life.

Iavor Lubomirov

After All This Time

After all this time I'm still alone
Found myself but not my home
My heart is full and my door is open
But damaged goods, I must be broken
Written in my desperate eyes
I cannot run from the lies
Past and present do collide
And knowing this, I will not hide.

Michelle McSorley

When Love Has Gone

A layer of dust, a single rose in bloom,
a salutary note - was all she left.
The air is still with scent and time - bereft
his eyes alight upon her quiet room.
The swish of skirts, her lace...the gentle swell
her bosom's grace - of those he missed the most,
her smiles replaced impassioned rows. Her boasts,
her playfulness - a tease; she knew him well.
What fated tryst had fashioned wrong
his wanting her - submit to love? He crushed
its growth, while tempered conversations blushed.
He thought he knew her strengths, her mind; so strong!
Her passion fuels his pain, he craves her spark,
her taunts when thoughts of love descend to dark.

Mary Lidia Evans

The Round Of Wrongs

Two wrongs make hate,
The first is a mistake,
The second is hazard,
Its twin is blame,
To wrong is to err,
Not my fault is said,
Excuse me, pardon,
Politeness is made,
To wrong for cause,
Soliciting hate,
Posters, papers, letters,
All sent,
To right is to love,
Except in extremes,
Where madness ensues,
And governs with hate.
Two wrongs make waste.

Keith Chalmers

Nature's Call

The wind howling Gods melody
a butterfly retreating, so gracefully
the rain pattering, rugged leaves
the whispering grass, elegantly pleads
for mercy from the crunching cow
the robotic ant, the farmers plough.

A robin so young, flew the nest
a grazing mouse, comes to rest
the ancient oak, to shut his eyes
the stealing crow, graces with lies
the sun away for the night
the moon revamps the missing light.

David Thomas Cox

Returning Her To Rome

Night fell in Rome
as we once did.
I have returned
to what never left me,
As a ruin amongst ruins
a statue by statues
once magnificent
sculptured by architects
crafted lovingly
to be destroyed
then admired,
by Lovers in the Emperors new shoes.

I remembered her last words.
Watched lovers mow scarlet,
and became invisible to them
blanched against a colonnade
which held nothing but achromatic skies
and me until sunrise.
This is my requiem for you my love.
The promise fulfilled,
you rise across the Tiber
taking my prayers with you
on pastures where you answered them
seven years ago in Rome,
Oh my love - we are home.

Antony Owen

Whirlpool

On harsh October days, your hazel eyes ignite
And light my footstep falls
As frayed nerve-endings tingle with delight,
Under a yellow neon light,
Or reflected in the panes of rain-flecked autumn days
I stand transfixed, amazed
That you would heed my explanations
While all around, whole nations
Fail to comprehend my awe.

And in that moment, when your hand turns to mine,
I glimpse a vision and I seek to bind it
Forever in my brain,
Refrains of half-forgotten love-songs
Jumble through my head
And I gaze, anew, at you and wonder
That upon such bliss I'd founder
As random atoms collide
And ride th' ensuing maelstrom
Locked together for all time.

Pat Ryan

The Memories

The memories fade, as the day gets older
The sorrow brightens with each day that you hold her
Close to you, close to your heart.
This moment, that moment, the moment you met
That day, this day, you'll never forget her.
There's one thing that keeps you apart.

A few days left, a few hearts broken
A few more hours till your last words are spoken
They can do more but choose to turn the other way
Those life pills, her dying day.

She used to pick you up when you were down
You always liked it when she was around
10 years ago to the day, she was nearly taken away
Nearly broken.
They fixed her up like she was an old work of art
Took an artery from her leg and sowed it to her heart
A bit like the memories she has of you
Sown eternally into her, close to her, close to you.

A few days left, a few hearts broken
A few less hours with the time they have stolen
They can do more but choose to ignore her pleas
The core of her soul begging on old knees.

Life's so negative; you're only relative,
Not much more that you can do
They're so full of it, there really pushing it,
They don't care how much this is hurting you.
I do.

Laura Bunn

Getting To Know You

I hear my neighbour through the walls
His frustrated, urgent calls
I hear his wife run down the stairs
Yelling like she has no cares
I hear their whispered words at night
Switching off the bedside light
I hear them slamming doors and shouting
Standing in the street and pouting
I hear her sobbing from afar
Him on the driveway with his car
I hear him saying his goodbyes
Her watching him with streaming eyes.

Charlie Middlemass

Crazy Wars

Dawn breaks and the earth quakes;
With the thought of war on the horizon.
The people in charge; shouldn't be at large
But of course their antics are not surprising
One is the leader of the labour party
The other is THE PRESIDENT with a swagger like JIM HARDY.
Looking for SADDAM'S arms for his ego to bolster
He just has to look down at the smoking gun in his holster.
Deep down TONY knows its all baloney
But he needs the support of the good old US of A
And has to play the role of the fool and the phoney
9/11 bit into the core; now it's time to even the score
The old pride dented and hurt it's time now for a savage retort.
After SEPTEMBER the 11th they were so lo sing their stature
They were loosing face
Strike back in anger and we'll make excuses
For the carnage and the disgrace.

Dessie Carabine

11

This is the sword, I am the new king
Working with dangerous people,
Willing to listen to the fireworks
Where each letter is replaced by another.

Few books today are forgivable,
Careful readings reveal a tunnel
But others show heavenly objects.
We put thirty spokes together and call it a wheel.

The treatment of carefully selected patients
Coincides with the Eros of divine Plato
 Becoming a social being with no taste for the pleasures.
Suffer it not any more.

In the house that smiles
Growing older, I learn all the time,
Disliking and pursuing, avoiding and rejecting
Because I despair of arriving.

John Blackburn

Every Time I See You

Every time I see you
My heart begins to flutter
But as I approach to talk to you
I suddenly begin to stutter
I go off into a world of my own
Not knowing what I am saying
Just wanting to be with you
Hoping and praying
I wish I would have the courage
To go and ask you out but it's the age
Gap that I am worried about
Your 13 in a few months time
You'll have just become a teen
But as I approach my next birthday
I'll be sweet 16
I really know it is love I'm feeling
No it's not a lie
For you I'd do anything maybe even die
Cos you are the love of my life
Forever faithful and true
If it wasn't for the age gap
I'll surely will be with you.

Georgina Blyth

Forces

The battle is getting hotter
And fear of the unknown makes me wonder -
Will I win or will I lose
When I'm face to face with my foes?
I'm not sure how I'll cope
But I never lose hope
And put my trust in the Lord
To help me carry this heavy load.

I rise to face another terrible day
Many bridges to burn on my way,
Life at times can be hard
But for every trying man is a reward.
I'm anticipating the repercussions
Coz every action has a reaction.
Anxiety is eating at me
As I'm dying to be free.

I'm up against evil forces
Practising different strokes
For different folks,
But in life there're no guarantees
Coz the future's not for me to foresee.
Well this is how life goes
There're the good times and the flaws
But who knows where my destiny lies
Except the Man who sits on high.

Nothing ever happens before its time
But who knows when the fruit's ripe,
I'm not a rebel without a cause
It's hell when you push me off course.
I'm not here to obey another's thoughts.

Joseph Nthini

Follow The Rainbow

Just follow the rainbow way up in the sky,
It brings forth such happiness for you and I,
It's a beautiful rainbow, just follow that dream,
Then you'll realise your rainbow is just what it seems.

Just follow the rainbow
To the end of your life
You will find such happiness,
And you will forget all the strife.

It's a beautiful rainbow a world without end,
It brings forth all memories, also all your friends,
The end of the rainbow, is a world full of peace,
When all of your pain and suffering will cease.

Rainbows end is where you'll be,
When you leave this life, you will be set free,
A beautiful place, filled with such love,
And with God's blessing up above.

The little bridge of time is there,
Cross over it, for dreams to share,
A life on a rainbow forever will be,
As pure in love, as eternity.

An island of dreams, that I know will come true,
An island of dreams, that I belong to me and you,
Just follow the rainbow way up in the sky,
And there you'll find such happiness for you and I.

Barbara Holme

The Bennett's Old Boatstore

A Market Street stroll and there, on The Cleave,
The Bennett's Old Boatstore faces the seas.
From May 'til September (when emmets leave)
Inside and outside repast at your ease.

Abandon the drudgery, end the hike,
Set down the tools, surrender to leisure.
Sup, chew and chat with Francesca and Mike
In an hour of convivial pleasure.

Meet without meat and mix without batter,
Music cool and Mokarabia hot.
No chips on china, paper or platter,
Risotto, Roskilly's, a veggie's lot.

Food in a gallery, art in a caff,
Hokey pokey, Purdy pasty and Blake.
Presley and Formby sing classical naff
And Boaty's with toasties, Caufield with cake.

Defense de fumer, smoke at your peril
But smile at the crumbs of celebrity,
Including Kingsand's Basil and Sybil,
Our hosts of the Cleaveside community.

Sit with the sweet peas, ignore the plastic.
Sail away, dreamer, with boats in the bay.
Sip both your coffee and dreams fantastic.
Safe on the horizon, the working day.

Jim Ravenhill

124

Cheerfulness

Try to be cheerful, whatever your lot
For its far better to be, rather than not
As cheerfulness is contagious you see
And you can obtain it without a fee!

Try to pay compliments, never complain
Always look to oneself, rather than blame
Gratitude and appreciation go hand in hand
When all of this you understand.

Strive to live a good life
Where everything is rife
It helps to oil the wheels of life
And therefore avoid strife.

Doing good is the chief matter
And this is the seed, which try to scatter
Then cheerfulness you will embrace
All else will go, without a trace.

Its always the doormat-not the mountains
Upon which you trip
But the little things we will surmount
And therefore get a grip.

Cheerfulness is a saving grace
Like courage, makes us bold
When the realisation this we know
Everything else will just unfold.

Gillian Morgan

The Way You Make Me Feel

I hate the way you stare at me,
the way you make me feel.

I hate the way you laugh at me,
the way you stand an giggle.

I hate the way you think you can mess me about,
the way you shout at me.

I hate the way you boss me about,
the way you make me feel small.

I hate the way you make me cry,
the way you toss me aside.

I hate the way you expect me to do everything for you.

I hate the fact you think you're right,
the way you never care.

I hate the way you treat me,
the way you always lie.

I hate the way you think you can always read my mind.

I think the thing I hate the most,
Is that deep down,
I don't hate you,
Not a little bit,
Not nearly,
Not at all.

Laura Edge

A Good Day

I woke up this morning,
Stretching and a yawning;
The songbirds they were calling,
And the sunshine it was roaring.
I got up, got dressed, I went for a walk,
No wind, no breeze, trees steady as a rock,
Has time stopped?
Is this a wind up, are there any batteries in the clock.
I reached the end of town, sat down upon the ground,
No noise, no sound, no living creature to be found,
As I sit there wondering if all is o.k.
I lift up my head and see two magpies at play,
And with a smile I think, Hey,
Could today be a good day.

As the afternoon draws near,
Still no life, nothing to fear;
Although my thoughts are so unclear,
Could this be the best day of my year?
I stood up, gazed round, before I wandered back to town,
Who's that woman I see, smiling like a clown;
Have I been crowned?
Is this paradise, or is this Heaven that I've found;
She passes me by, smiling and acting shy,
I call her back, no response, no reply.
Then suddenly the sky turns grey,
Voices in my head saying walk this way,
Step off the path, onto the highway, oh no,
Damn, today was a good day.

Rodney Kane

Little Bells

These little bells that do not ring
They show their heads around late spring.

These little bells that do not chime
Stand like soldiers in a line.

These little bells that do not peel
Carpet woods and dale and hill.

These little bells that aren't quite blue
Look so dramatic showing through.

They may not ring a tune we know
But bluebells set our hearts aglow.

Susan Whitfield

The Window

I see all from this pain,
The passers they go by.
The roads are moving with metal waste,
The floods fall down today.

Shine steals my eyes,
Black dots stain my view,
Penguin men are approaching, ready to unite the world,
Stare comes in to contact.

A military man, fall to the ground,
Now stand to attention,
The base is yours after all,
The world is yours.
Why retreat and surrender?

Dismal pictures of creatures,
Appear to eat the sun,
The mass to big, can't hide.

Too late the dam has broke,
The monsters are as many,
When they join, strength is too strong.

Bang, Bang
The guns have flown,
The bullets trail of light,
Defeated, Cold,
But their artillery has gone.

A fire blazes,
One penguin comes out to play,
The gold is far, but will be found,
If the colours never ever fade.

Gareth Evans

Waves

The heave and swell upon the restless sea,
And hurl themselves against the rocky coasts;
They roll white-crested smoothly as can be
And mingle with the bathing, swimming hosts.

Invisible to everything on earth,
They travel through the ether in a flash
And bring to ears and eyes the sounds of mirth,
And subjects which are serious or trash.

Hails and farewells are present every day:
We greet and part with hand in quivering pose;
When distance hinders words that we would say,
A waving hand expresses all of those.

So sea and air and people all combine
In making waves all different in their way;
Their universal use we may define
According to the purpose that they play.

H J Griffin